DIARIES OF A FEMALE
REAL ESTATE INVESTOR

Diaries of a Female Real Estate Investor
Learn How a Single Mom Went From Over $80k in Debt to a Multi-Million Dollar Real Estate Portfolio

Farrah Ali

Published by Game Changer Press, LLC DBA Game Changer Publishing

ISBN: 978-1-7365491-8-6

www.PublishABestSellingBook.com

DEDICATION

In honor of my grandmother, who passed away before my birth. Her strong character, loving nature, and independence left such a lasting impression that even after her passing, her descendants were able to benefit from her inspiration. A widow who single handedly managed the family business while raising seven children on her own.

DOWNLOAD YOUR FREE GIFTS

Read This First

Just to say thanks for buying and reading my book, I would like to give you a 100% bonus gift for FREE, no strings attached!

To Download Now, Visit:
www.FarrahAli.org/freegift

DIARIES OF A FEMALE REAL ESTATE INVESTOR

Learn How a Single Mom Went From Over $80k in Debt
to a Multi-Million Dollar Real Estate Portfolio

Farrah Ali

www.PublishABestSellingBook.com

Foreword

AS A SMALL CHILD, I remember my dad telling me many times that I could do anything I wanted to do or be anything that I wanted to be. I grew up with this belief. My dad was an entrepreneur, and he was a trailblazer in every sense of the word. He passed away when I was a teenager, but I always carried this belief with me.

However, many decades later, what I found in the real world was that everyone didn't think like him. I started and grew two successful businesses, both of which were in male dominated fields, and I can't say that it was always easy.

Hindsight is a funny thing. I didn't realize how much his words would shape my journey as a real estate investor. When I began reading this book written by successful investor Farrah Ali, one of the first things that caught my eye was the major influence her own entrepreneurial grandmother had over her own life. This was true even though she passed away before she was born.

I realize that not everyone is fortunate enough to have someone like this in their life. In fact, you may not always have the support of your friends and family as you start your own journey.

That's why this book is so empowering for female investors. Farrah has been where you are. You get to learn firsthand from a successful woman who began her journey much like many other people, and that was a journey with many challenges.

Despite those initial challenges and the ones that were yet to come, she purchased 25 rentals and built a multi-million-dollar portfolio of single-family homes in just four years. This has allowed her to become financially free in an extremely short period of time. She did this as a single mother with two children and a full-time job (with a 2-hour commute).

How did she do it? You will find the answers in her story within the pages of this inspiring book.

In my experience, the one thing that sets successful female investors apart from those that aren't successful is their mindset. Farrah's ability to master her own mindset and move past her fear is evident throughout this book.

It's likely that as you're reading this book, you aren't sure that you have what it takes to succeed in this business. I want you to know that you do, and you can. You have everything you need to succeed within you. Know that confidence and resilience are muscles you build over time.

What you might be lacking is the "how-to" piece. That's exactly what you will find within these pages—Farrah's roadmap for success. You can model her success by following the strategies and tips detailed in the book. These are the same ones she still uses in her own business today.

There are a lot of great lessons here, including how she researched neighborhoods, the different ways she structured her deals, and why a lack of cash in your bank account is never an excuse to delay getting started. You will learn about working with both commercial and private money lenders as well as working with partners.

One of the things I loved most about this book is what Farrah learned from making lots of offers on properties she didn't get. This experience made her a better, more confident investor. Despite the fact it wasn't much fun at the time, she is truly grateful for all the experiences, both good and bad, along the way.

Here's another thing I love about this book. Being the smart businesswoman that she is, Farrah has kept her W-2 job so that she never has to use her rental income for monthly expenses. This has allowed her to take the cash flow from her rentals and the cash she earns from her flips and wholesale deals to pay down her rental properties much more quickly.

Farrah Ali shows you a proven method not only for building a successful real estate investing business but also for overcoming any fears you have about your ability to succeed as a real estate investor. Anyone can do it with the right mindset and the right mentors. She is incredibly generous when it comes to sharing her time, her knowledge, and her support. Farrah is a true role model for all investors.

As a woman who has spent more than 20 years in this field, I can tell you that I spent a lot of time trying to get a seat at the table in the "good old boys club" when I was often one of the few women in the room.

Female role models were scarce then, and surprisingly still far and few between today. Whether you are just getting started or you're a seasoned investor, this book is a must-read. Farrah's journey is inspiring, and she is a shining example of what is possible for any woman that is willing to put in the time and the work needed to succeed in this business.

For all the women out there reading this book, know that you no longer need a seat at the table in the "good old boy's club." We've built our own table!

Sharon Vornholt
Creator of the Louisville Gal's Real Estate Blog and Let's Talk Real Estate Investing Podcast and Founder of Probate Investing Simplified

Table of Contents

Introduction

IT WAS JUNE 15, 2009. I distinctly remember sitting in my Nissan Rogue at the Jewel grocery store parking lot in Westmont, Illinois, looking left to right and front to back, wondering if he spotted me. My body was full of adrenaline, and I sat there wondering what the hell just happened in the last 20 minutes.

I was being chased by a gray Dodge Minivan. I was not exactly sure why I was being chased or how it was going to end. I just knew I had to drive as fast as I could, make as many turns as I could make, while simultaneously trying not to hurt anyone or get flagged by the police. I had my seven-year-old son in the back seat, and I kept looking in the rearview mirror to see if he was safe. I couldn't help but notice his reaction. I remember him saying, "Mommy, he is getting closer. Go faster!" While turning his head to the back windshield every couple of seconds.

It was my spouse chasing me! I had just told him I wanted a separation and that I was moving away. It was an extremely hard decision, but I felt like I was out of options. My older son was in my husband's car, watching this car chase play out. I thought to myself how these traumatizing memories would forever be etched in their minds.

I recently signed a lease on a new home, and I was trying to reach there. Come to think of it, maybe that was why he was following me, to see where I was going, but I wasn't ready for him to know. At least, not for the time being.

After waiting about 20 minutes in the parking lot, I started making my way cautiously towards my new home. The home was empty except for a couple of mattresses, some food, and a table to eat on, but it was still a home. It was my home, and I was grateful to have a roof over my head even though I was down to a couple of hundred dollars in my bank account after using nearly my entire savings of $3,200 for the security deposit and 1st month's rent.

I left a 10-year marriage. I sacrificed the house, furniture, and other belongings I accumulated over the past ten years. I had no real plan on what I was going to do moving forward and had very little support because my entire family was living out of state, and I did not want to inconvenience anyone. Although I walked away with little material belongings, I had my children by my side along with faith in myself. I didn't know how, when, or where—I just knew I was going to take it one moment at a time.

I knew my decision to rebuild my life would come with consequences. It would be hard for the kids trying to adjust to the new place, coping with the separation, and possibly having to go to a new school. They had attended the same private school for years. As a mother, I chose what was best for them–any child support payments would go toward keeping them in their school.

When bad things happen, it is natural to wonder, "Why me?" It is human nature to look for something or someone to blame. Each person's struggle is unique, and some hardships may be more intense than others. The one thing I do know is that if I did not go through these challenges, it would not have brought me to where I am today, to who I am today, and with whom I surround myself today. If not for these circumstances, I may have never discovered the one thing that has ultimately taken care of my family and me and set us up for the rest of our lives–REAL ESTATE!

Hi, my name is Farrah Ali, and for most of my life, I have searched for life's purpose, especially my own. I have noticed life's toughest questions usually come up during challenging or emotional times and that most negative feelings can be directly attributed to money or lack of it. I want to share the techniques and strategies I have spent years learning and perfecting to help you change your circumstances and build a brighter future. Sure, money is a big piece of the puzzle, but *time* is the real key. The ability to do what you want, when you want, is the best measure of true success and happiness.

During my journey, I realized that changing my actions would result in changed outcomes and thus result in a change in my emotions. I took my first significant step when I separated from my husband in 2009. That decision accelerated a series of other changes that ultimately altered the trajectory of my life.

There have been numerous times that I have shared my successes and my stories. However, I've always felt that I have so much more to share. Now is that time. I want people to get the entire picture, not just the cliff notes version, because, to truly have a good understanding, it's essential to know the highs and lows and everything in between. Navigating your way through success should be real and raw. You need someone to give you an accurate representation of what goes into it. It's like looking in awe at a work of art but never seeing everything the artist experienced to get the paint on the canvas—the good, the bad, and the ugly.

I remember the first time I was asked to share the story of my first real estate deal. It was a single-family home in a small suburb of Chicago. I had to go on stage at a seminar in front of more than 300 attendees. I did not understand why anyone would want to listen to someone who had only one investment property. Other investors on stage had anywhere from 5 to 100+ properties. I tried to get out of it because I was embarrassed I only had one rental home, and why would anyone want to listen to an amateur when it came to real estate? None of my excuses worked, so there I was on stage talking about my circumstances and how I was able to purchase that property with no money of my own.

The situation is very different now, but when I started investing, I was approximately $80K in debt from a combination of school loans and credit card debt. To make the situation even worse, I had absolutely no savings. Here I was, a single mom with the sole financial responsibility for two children, in addition to being the residential custodial parent.

Fortunately, I had a stable job that took care of the day to day expenses and a decent credit score, so I had those two blessings working in my favor. People were amazed that I could still purchase an investment home despite all my debt and no savings.

I walked the audience through the property's particulars: The purchase price, rehab amount, what it appraised for, and how much monthly rental income I was receiving.

When I was done speaking, I was so relieved that it was over. I walked off the stage with my sweaty palms and a sense of relief. I went from an embarrassment level of 8 down to a 2. To my surprise, people actually clapped, but people usually always clap after leaving the stage, so I didn't think anything of it.

After my testimonial, there was a short 15-minute break. As I walked down the hallway, the seminar attendees, mainly women, started bombarding me with questions and comments. They were congratulating me left, and right and some even had tears in their eyes. I was so perplexed. I couldn't understand what the big deal was. Then I began to understand when I had multiple women and men telling me how inspiring I was. Many were in similar situations, whether it was divorce, massive debt, or parents who were raising children solo. I had inspired them, and they were interested in learning more about how I overcame it all and how they could do the same.

That was when I understood it wasn't about me. It was about them. That day, my story gave people hope. If it worked for me, it could work for them too. That day, several people began taking their first steps towards change, and today they are living in success.

I realized the power of telling one meaningful story. It held a promise of a better future, and if I inspired just one person, then it was all worth it.

The intention of this book is two-fold. It gives me a way to express myself in a way that allows me to share my experiences and stories with a broader audience, so perhaps it may inspire more people and bring them one step closer to achieving their dreams.

Whether you're skeptical of real estate or have little to no experience, this book should have something for everyone. It will cover some common myths, great strategies, and tips and teach you how to scale up to do as many deals as you desire. It will inspire you to take action because it doesn't matter how much money you have. It doesn't matter what type of credit you have, or even how much time you have. There is a solution for everyone. Some may go at a faster pace than others, but the most important thing is to get started. You will soon see that one action leads to another and then another. Before you know it, you can go from having $80k in debt to a multi-million dollar portfolio and enough passive income to replace your current income and much more!

How To Use This Book:

I have been around thousands of real estate investors over the years, and I've noticed some common traits in those who are successful versus those who are not. I'm going to share those with you so that your chances of succeeding are much higher and at a faster rate. Also, I've noticed that many people don't understand the bigger picture. They are too involved in the details too soon (which is just as important, but at the right time). This was my issue as well when I began. Although I got my first deal fairly quickly, it took me a while to purchase the second. Had I understood the bigger picture, I would have been able to identify opportunities that I didn't initially see as opportunities because my mind was not as expanded as it is today.

Throughout the book, I will share **Real** examples. These are actual numbers of the properties I personally have in my investment portfolio. You should be able to grasp the concept and style of investing I use. It is imperative to learn it this way because even if the market goes down 25 to 30 percent, you will still be in a good place financially. I have met many investors using other methods, but I have not seen the returns and profitability at a rate anywhere near the way investing was taught to me. It is true that you learn by gaining experience, but learning from other people's experience can be just as effective.

Many people invest in real estate, but it isn't as lucrative because they have their own ideas of what investing is. For example, buying a pretty house at retail prices is not my definition of investing. A sound investment is getting monthly net cash flow and having equity in the property, and that equity is realized as soon as the purchase is made.

And yes, it's true! It doesn't matter what circumstance you are in:

- Bad credit
- No money
- Lack of time - a full-time job
- Single parent
- No education

There is a solution for everyone! The question is, how badly do you want it? Throughout this book, I will share some valuable myths and tips that I learned through my journey. At times I will go into some of my personal stories to give context to the circumstances I was dealing with. These stories are important because they are a part of my real estate journey.

So let's get started!

CHAPTER ONE

What is Your Problem?

IT TOOK ME MANY YEARS to figure out what I really wanted in life. The things I thought I wanted didn't feel as enjoyable once I acquired them. Ultimately, I realized what it was that I was after. It wasn't necessarily a luxury car, a nice purse, fine dining, a big home, or any one thing in particular. I realized all my goals were based on trying to obtain a certain feeling. I was able to discern what actions resulted in the feelings of fulfillment and contentment and which resulted in feelings that were short-lived.

I was born in the city of Chicago and raised in the western suburbs of Chicago. My parents got married in India, and shortly after that, they came to the United States as immigrants. My father was extremely skilled in mathematics and was invited to the United States to study and work, where he graduated with a Masters in Engineering. My grandparents, on both sides of my family, passed away before I was even born. My parents had no support and had to build their life from scratch, just like many immigrants do. It took some time to build, especially while raising four daughters. We were raised in, what I would call, a hardworking middle-class family. They earned every single dollar they had. Perhaps being raised in this environment is where my work ethic came from.

It's interesting how some childhood memories stand out, and others just seem to fade away over time.

I recall watching television episodes, and there would be scenes of people dining out at nice fancy restaurants, and I remember thinking that fine dining was only for the rich. As a child, I did not identify myself in the category of "rich" because our family would rarely dine out. My mom believed home-cooked meals were healthier and also believed that it was beneficial to spend any extra money on family vacations.

Fast forward to after my divorce, and I remember I was so excited the day I first went to a fine dining restaurant—one of those restaurants that you spend more than $100 per person. I finally got to feel "rich." The meal was delicious, and I was surrounded by what seemed to be other wealthy people, but over time, the feeling started to fade with every restaurant I went to. I was getting bored, and the food wasn't always as great as I imagined it to be. That is when I realized that we conjure up stories in our heads, and we learn reality by experiencing. Life is a process of learning about ourselves, and it can take decades for us to learn who we really are and what we really want. Unfortunately, some people go through their entire lives never really discovering who they are. They are so distracted by the constant bombardment of propaganda, media, and what others think that they live their lives in ignorance.

I want to share what took me more than three decades to figure out—a term I call Intentional Consciousness. It's when you pay attention to what truly excites or drives YOU, and you intentionally work towards that goal. You pay attention to how you spend your time and resources, and if it does not align with your goals, you eliminate or reduce those activities from your life.

A sense of fulfillment is what most of us strive for. If you have ever truly experienced feeling fulfilled, you will realize that it is a feeling that never goes away. At times the intensity of the feeling fluctuates, but it's always there like a song playing in the background. The nice part is that you have control of the volume. When you are immersed in feelings of fulfillment, situations change in life that bring you more of the same feeling. You will notice the frequency of interacting with negative people and negative situations will diminish.

You must be wondering what this has to do with real estate investing. Hang tight. I am getting there.

Remember, I mentioned I would provide you with a short-cut to success in real estate investing. The FIRST thing you need to do is identify what you want or what you are after. The path becomes so much clearer and quicker when you have goals in mind, and in this context, the first step to your goals is to identify which feelings you want to change.

When I talk about what feelings to change, I am not referring to visitors. Visitors are those feelings that are short-lived and don't really stay long enough to have an impact on your life. For example, let's say you went on a first date and really enjoyed it, but the other party showed no interest in a second date. This may result in feelings of disappointment but is usually temporary because it has to do with one experience. It wasn't a significant amount of time and energy invested in the first date. The feelings we need to focus on are the ones we feel almost daily, which impact our lives, our decisions and can consume or drain us.

I will walk you through the process of three feelings I consistently felt that I knew I had to change. You may identify with one or more of the same feelings, or you may have a completely different set of feelings, but the process will be the same. The process is as follows.

- Identify the undesired feelings.
- Determine the life events that cause me to feel that way.
- Identify solutions to eliminate those unwanted feelings.

Undesired Feeling #1 - The monotony of living a routine lifestyle and the stress of being on someone else's schedule:

I distinctly remember the feeling of having the same daily routine of going to work five days a week, coupled with the stress of having to make it to work exactly on time. My former boss was strict when it came to being punctual. If I was even the slightest bit late, it would reflect negatively on my annual performance review. It wasn't easy making it to work on time. I had to try to balance getting as much sleep as I could with the little ones waking up throughout the night and trying to gauge the traffic for that day so that I could time it right.

My commute was over an hour, so it was quite challenging, but being even 5 minutes late resulted in a warning.

Undesired Feeling #2 - Never being able to save money. Nothing to fall back on:

I first started working part-time while I was attending high-school. Although I didn't mind working, the routine of going to work for all these years didn't feel right. I felt I was putting in all this time, but the balance in my bank account wasn't anything substantial. I tried to take a small percentage of my paycheck and put it in savings, but there was always some sort of unexpected expense that would eat up the savings.

Undesired Feeling #3 - Fear of not being able to be a good, responsible parent; what if I didn't have enough:

Being a single mother and receiving no child support for a couple of years was a scary feeling. How was I going to support my two kids entirely on my own? I knew the expenses would grow as they got older, but the income from my job would not grow at the same rate. What if I couldn't keep up with the expenses? What if they wanted to join an extracurricular activity and I couldn't afford it? The possibility of not being able to fulfill my role as a parent made me incredibly insecure.

There had to be a solution to all of these unwanted feelings?

The cornerstone to all these feelings was the lack of one resource—money. Earning more money wasn't necessarily the only solution that would help my situation, but it was a significant one. I spent hours researching on the internet and reading books on how to become wealthy, and what I learned was the key to building real wealth was earning PASSIVE INCOME! The king of all passive income was owning real estate. It's worked for centuries. Naturally, the next step was to start reading all I could about real estate, and as my knowledge grew, so did my hope for the future.

Little did I know, four years from the moment I started my real estate journey, I would have 25 rental properties in my portfolio and over 30 partnership deals in many other real estate transactions. I was able to acquire properties at a much faster rate than some of the other investors who had been investing in real estate for decades.

The best part was that I could purchase the homes with very little or no cash of my own and make ridiculously great returns. What took some investors 20 years to accomplish, I was able to do in only a few years. I am so grateful for this journey, and I'm excited to share all of it with you.

Real Estate Myth

1. You need 20% down-payment to purchase an investment property.

It's possible not to have to use any of your own money to invest in a property as long as the cash flow and equity meet the lender's requirements. There are private money lenders who will lend 100% for purchase and rehab. Other lenders, such as hard money lenders, will loan around 90% purchase and 100% rehab. Rates and the amount of the loan vary based on the lender.

Real Estate Investing Tip

Set aside some funds to invest in real estate education and a networking and support group. This is key in being able to avoid making any significant mistakes. Most novice investors who don't have a support system end up making costly mistakes. It is important to invest in the right course. There are many out there, but only a few that have consistently successful results.

CHAPTER TWO

What is Real Estate Investing? What We Think It Is Versus What It Actually Is

THERE ARE MANY FORMS of Real estate investing. You can invest in a piece of land, residential single-family homes, multi-units, apartment/condo buildings, commercial buildings, strip malls, and new construction. My experience is solely with residential single-family homes and multi-units. Although similar concepts can be applied to all, our focus will be on residential single-family homes and multi-units with anywhere between 2-4 units per property.

When people ask me what I do, I tell them I'm in real estate. 90% of them assume I am a real estate agent. I am not sure if that is because there are more real estate agents than investors or if they just assume it based on my gender. I did have someone comment that they thought I was an agent because it was rare for women to invest in real estate, although I know many women who invest in real estate and are quite successful.

The difference between being a real estate agent and a real estate investor is that a real estate agent takes the real estate licensing course and must pass the exam to get licensed to either list homes for sale or be an agent for a buyer looking to purchase a home. Their compensation is commission. Once the purchase is complete and the commission is paid, the transaction is over.

A real estate investor purchases a property either for a short term or long term and either rents it to tenants or improves the property and sells it for a profit.

This may seem like very basic knowledge for some of you, but you would be surprised how many people I have come across who are confused between the two. I thought it would be appropriate to mention it to make sure everyone understands the difference.

Another false notion that many people seem to have is that you need to have a significant amount of money to invest in properties. This is so far from the truth. You really don't need much cash to start investing. Let me lay out exactly what my situation was when I invested in my first property.

My personal profile at the start of investing:

Status - Divorced and a single mom of two boys with majority financial responsibility
Gender- Female
Real Estate Experience - None
Home - Single-family - Mortgage payment of 1800 per month

Job- Underwriting Manager at an Insurance company making $80,000 annual salary

Credit Score - 730

School debt - 75,000

Credit card debt - $13.000

Savings - None

401k - $20,000

Child support - $250 per child per month (total $500 per month)

I list my situation prior to investing because, as you can see, I had $0 savings and a significant amount of debt. Some of you may be wondering why I came in with $0 savings even though I worked a majority of my life. When I got married at the age of 22, I wasn't mature enough to realize that the decisions we make have a huge impact on our lives and circumstances. At 22, I thought I knew it all and ignored the advice I received from elders. I felt they didn't understand me, but I realized years later that life experience is more valuable than I thought. When my parents advised me repeatedly not to marry him, I didn't take it seriously enough. It wasn't because he was a bad person, but they knew that the mindset and culture would clash. I married regardless and paid the price. Little did I know that I would deal with situations where I didn't have access to bank accounts where a significant amount of my salary was deposited. Being raised in America, I found it very odd, but I guess some people are big on having complete control of the finances.

Over the years, the financial situation continued to get worse even though I was getting promotions at work with pay increases. Poor financial decisions were being made to the point that there was so much injustice I just couldn't bear it anymore. I didn't realize how much impact a spouse's decisions can make. He decided to stop working full-time and try out new construction. I tried to persuade him to keep his job and do real estate part-time until our financial circumstances improved. We had two very young kids and had credit card debt we needed to pay off. We still needed stability. His friends, who were going to be his future business partners, had a certain influence on him that I didn't have. He chose to officially end his full-time career. That decision had such an impact on our financial situation that we never recovered.

I don't blame anyone for my situation. I chose my spouse, so I had to try to work with what I had, but at the age of 22, I was still discovering who I was. I made a decision based on the intellectual, mental, and emotional capacity I had at the time. He made decisions based on his. We all make mistakes, and it is part of the process. If we learn from them and improve, it's all worth it.

One of the most common questions I get asked is, "If you had no money, how did you invest with no money down?"

There are various lenders out there that will lend 100% of your purchase and rehab cost. There are also other hard money lenders who lend in the vicinity of 90% purchase and 100% rehab costs, as well as a combination of other options suitable to your situation.

I personally went the private money lender route because I had no access to cash of my own.

Why do these private money lenders loan 100% of purchase and rehab?

Lenders are in the business of making money. They have cash on hand that they want to put to work. They also may have funds sitting in an IRA account they can lend from. The returns from doing this are usually greater and more stable than investing those funds in the stock market.

Why would they take the risk of loaning 100%?

Private money lenders lend based on the asset and whether the risk and profitability ratios meet the standards. If the investor has a good deal on their hands, the loan is usually approved.

Note that before I started investing, I did not have any experience with real estate investing. Yet, I was still able to obtain a loan for the full purchase and rehab because I met the lender's requirements. I had a property that had great potential for cash flow and equity. I could refinance the loan and pay the lender back once the rehab process was completed.

In this scenario, I was able to refinance because I had a stable W-2 income using the residential loan process. Even if you don't have a W-2, you can still refinance using a commercial loan. Commercial loan rates are slightly higher, but there is no reason why you shouldn't do a deal just because you are getting a loan with a slightly higher percentage.

Some of you might be confused at this point, so let me break it down a little more. When you purchase a property using cash, the lender provides the funds at closing. The additional funds for the rehab are provided to you directly to use for fixing up the property.

Once the property rehab is completed, you rent to a tenant and start the refinance process with a different bank(residential or commercial) so that you can pay off the private money lender. The bank gets an appraisal done to secure the property's value and grants you a loan, usually based on the house's appraisal. This can be a 5-30 year loan (depending on what the banks offer) at competitive interest rates.

Once the refinance is complete, the original lender is paid off in full, and now you have an investment rental property that will give you net cash flow each month. There is a monthly mortgage payment you will pay to the new bank, but you use the tenant's rent money to pay the mortgage.

If you don't fully understand yet, don't worry. We will be going through some real case studies to help you understand the process using actual numbers, but the point I would like you to take from this is that you don't need any of your own money to invest in properties.

Another question I get asked frequently is how do you do it? How do you find the time being a single parent with two kids with a full-time career?

My answer has always been one word: Prioritize. We all get to choose how we want to spend the 24 hours we have in the day.

We all eat, sleep, shower/groom, which takes a significant portion of our day. Let's just say all of our daily "tasks" consume a total of 10 hours per day. We are now left with about 14 hours. So how do we spend our 14 hours per day? Most of us work an average of 8 hours per day and have an average commute of 2 hours per day for 5 days per week. This leaves us with 4 hours in which we have to fit in cooking, helping kids with homework, other household chores, etc.

If you can find 1-2 hours per day, you should have no issues succeeding in real estate. How do you find that time? Here are a few suggestions:

1. Cut down an hour of sleep, especially if you are sleeping for more than 8 hours.
2. Meal prep on the weekends so that you are spending no more than 45 minutes a day cooking on the weeknights.
3. Limit social activities with friends who don't help you grow.
4. Try to have your phone conversations while you are cooking or driving or doing other household chores. Use a Bluetooth headset so you are hands-free.
5. Hire a maid for cleaning. The time you would spend to clean is better spent investing in real estate knowledge and networking.
6. Turn your limited social activities into social activities with real estate investors. You will see that even your social time can be productive and fun.
7. Reach out to friends or family members for help with the kids.

8. Work from home if possible. You will save time on commuting, and that time can be allotted elsewhere. You can even throw some laundry in and get that started.

9. Get the kids involved. Go see a property with them and make it a family event.

10. Limit your TV and Netflix shows. You will have to sacrifice for a while, but making the right choices now will give you ample time in the future.

11. Listen to real estate podcasts or videos while you're doing chores or at the gym, or while driving. This can be used as learning time.

The point I am trying to make is that if you **really** want to do something, you can always find the time. Feeling like you don't have the time is a mental block. As you start working on the things you want to do, you will find that circumstances in your life begin to change to allow more time for what you begin to prioritize. You just need to start and stick with it for about three weeks, and you will begin to see the changes over time.

Real Estate Myth

2. I have no real estate experience, so I need to start with wholesaling.

I hear this phrase quite often, and it is completely false. Having little or no experience has nothing to do with the strategy you use. For example, I started with acquiring rentals for the first three years before

I did any wholesaling. The strategy you use is unique to your own situation and has nothing to do with experience.

Real Estate Investing Tip - While planning your investing goals, discuss your situation with someone who has already invested in real estate. The advice from an experienced investor may open up to possibilities that you haven't thought about. Make sure they have experience in the type of investing you are interested in.

CHAPTER THREE

How Do You Get Over Your Fear?

BREAKING INTO AN INDUSTRY that you have no experience in can feel intimidating. I didn't know where to begin. I had no close friends to guide me. I researched online, and there was a lot of information, but the research was increasingly confusing. I would read an article, but then the next article I read had conflicting information. I felt lost and didn't know where to turn. During my research, the book *Rich Dad Poor Dad* was recommended as a good read for new investors. That was an easy enough decision, so I ordered the book online.

I quickly read through the entire book as soon as I received it. The book was enjoyable and helpful because it helped me understand the investor mindset. I never realized that the mindset of an employee, entrepreneur, and investor was so different. I realized that I've been carrying an employee mindset and the first thing I needed to do was shift my mindset to an investor. Toward the end of the RDPD book, there was a coaching session offered. I was excited to call because naturally, that felt like the next step, but, at the time, I couldn't afford it. I was so excited to take the next step but didn't have the funds to pay for it.

Working on changing your mindset is definitely a process. I realized as circumstances appeared in my life, I would revert to my old ways of thinking. For example, when I realized I didn't have enough funds to pay for the course, I thought of other ways to make money and began working my way back towards an employee mindset. I thought about getting my MBA so that I could get a promotion. I applied to the NIU Executive MBA program and was on my way to a master's degree. I got a federal student loan, and my employer also helped cover some of the costs. It took me just under two years to finish the MBA program. During those two years, real estate was no longer on my mind. I was focused on completing my MBA and was looking forward to my huge pay increase once I graduated. It was June 2013, and I finally graduated! It wasn't easy working full time, being a single parent, and working on the MBA. I slept less, had very little social life, had to choose which family events I could skip without offending anyone. I don't think I ever turned on my television for those few years.

A few weeks after I graduated, I went to my boss and put in a proposal of the ideas I had to grow the business, the changes I would make to the department, and asked for a pay increase now that I had that MBA. She looked over the proposal and agreed that I should get an increase. Yes! Finally, I could afford all the extra things I wanted. The company gave me a 15% increase in salary, which I was very grateful for, but when I calculated what that would amount to, I realized it was only a few hundred dollars per paycheck. I guess I wasn't going to buy all the nice things I wanted. I hired tutors for the kids, and those extra wages disappeared quickly. Don't get me wrong, I don't regret getting the MBA. I learned a few things that I could use at work or in a business. I made great friends and felt a lot more confident in myself. Getting an MBA does have its perks; however, I realized it didn't do much for me financially. I was back to square one with the finances but a more confident and educated one.

After realizing that the paycheck to paycheck situation hadn't changed, I called the RDPD coaching program. I received an end of year bonus and decided to join the course. I joined and was super excited to start my real estate journey.

The coach assigned to me would meet with me via a weekly half-hour phone call. He asked me to go look at 100 properties. I didn't know where to start or what to look for.. How do I find an agent who knew about investing? What if I purchased something, and there was a major mechanical issue or foundation issue with the house? Even though I had a coach, I still felt alone. I asked him if he knew anyone local, and he didn't have anyone he could refer me to. He made one suggestion that helped. He asked me to join a local real estate group or an REIA (Real estate Investing Association). I decided to take his advice and started to search for some online.

I was intimidated to walk into an REIA meeting by myself, but I forced myself to get out of my comfort zone. The particular REIA I first chose made me feel somewhat uncomfortable. I felt like it was one of those groups that were less about learning real estate investing and more about getting other people to join the group. I guess they had some sort of multi-level marketing scheme. Quite honestly, it turned me off. I wanted to learn real estate investing, not try to bring in people. Then I decided to join a group that played the cashflow game, and there I met a newer investor who told me about some three-day event that was coming up the following weekend at a completely different REIA. He said it seemed like it would be helpful, so I said, sure, let's give it a shot, and that is where I found my 2nd home! Finally, exactly what I was looking for. It was Chicago REIA, they held their three-day conference for the first time in June 2014, and I was blown away with all the information I just learned. The guy who was putting on the presentation clearly knew his stuff. His name is Andrew Holmes, and he has done hundreds of real estate deals. Normally I would be skeptical when I hear those types of numbers, but he actually had the list of properties with the exact addresses to prove it.

I had been to a few seminars before, but I hadn't seen anything like this. After three intense days of mind-blowing information that I would never have learned on my own, I started to see the light and, at the same time, felt a strong intuition that this was the place I needed to be to succeed.

I know this chapter is about getting over your fears, but I wanted to share this very important experience. If you noticed, I had been to a few different groups or seminars before I stumbled across the one that produced results. I didn't give up and kept going. Most people would quit after a few uneventful experiences, but I believe if you are passionate about something, you should continue seeking until you find it. The nice thing is that you can save a significant amount of time researching where to log in. I can help lay out the path for you that will have you investing in real estate in no time! Now back to dealing with fear.

Fear usually presents when you don't have enough knowledge, have information overload, or can't distinguish between what information is credible. Think about a moment in your life, in the past, when you were fearful of something, and after learning and practicing it a few times, the fear slowly begins to disappear. Real estate investing is no different. Getting the RIGHT KNOWLEDGE is key! As you gain more and more knowledge, you will soon replace those feelings of fear with confidence. There is so much information out there, and it is difficult to follow along one path. I have met many people who have taken numerous courses, seminars, conferences and still have nothing to show for it.

You need to be around people who are actually producing results. The right knowledge and education are necessary, but it needs to be followed up with action. Having a network of people around you actively investing in real estate will increase your chances of producing results.

Real Estate Myth

3. I have bad credit, and no lender will work with me on my deal.

Many lenders out there are willing to lend to you based upon the deal presented and not your credit score. Many private lenders don't run your credit score. As long as you have a property that they feel will result in a successful transaction, you should get funded.

Real Estate Investing Tip - When reaching out to a lender, put together a lending proposal that includes the property address, some details regarding the property, the purchase price, the rehab amount, comparables, and your exit strategy. The proposal should be professional and well presented.

CHAPTER FOUR

My First Deal - Let's Walk Through This

WHEN I GOT MY FIRST DEAL under contract, I was overwhelmed with emotions. I thought to myself, *Wow, this actually works!* I was so excited, grateful, curious, and a bit scared (in a good way) for what was to come. It was time to put all of what I learned into action.

So you ask how I got my first deal under contract? Well, I ended up joining a course, and it's one of those courses that actually teaches you investing and has an amazing support system and mentors. One of the lessons I learned in class was to research areas and really get to know them street by street if possible. I chose about 8-10 suburbs in the Chicago area to research. I came across a small village called Lyons that I had never heard of before; it was in a good pocket, area-wise. I began to research further and found the crime rate to be fairly low. The schools were decent. Homeownership vs. rentals was at a good percentage. The average household income also fell into the category ideal for investments. In talking to a friend at work, he told me he grew up in Lyons. I was so excited, and I immediately set up a meeting with him the following day. He asked me why, and I told him I'd let him know at our meeting.

When I got home, I looked up a map of the town. I found a really nice one, so I went to Kinkos to print out a few copies that were of a decent size so that I could see the names of every street. I took three highlighters and a pen with me. The next day during our meeting, I had him go street by street. At the same time, I used the three different highlighters to categorize them as highly desirable streets to invest in, so-so areas, and then areas to stay away from which had frequent flood activity or crime. There was even an old quarry in the area that he told me to stay away from because the houses around it may have foundation issues.

Now that I had all the details of this map, I took a picture of it on my phone and emailed it to myself as well. As soon as I saw something come up for sale, I could look at the house's area and decide if I wanted to proceed all in a matter of five minutes.

This exercise was so useful because the very next property I got under contract was also in Lyons. I was able to act fast and knew my numbers from the templates provided to me in class.

Let's go over the details for my first property.

Property type - Two-story single-family brick home, two bedrooms and one bath, half-finished basement
Purchase price = $75,000
Rehab amount = $20,000

Holding costs = $6,000 (interest, utilities, taxes)

Appraisal after the property was rehabbed = $145,000

Lease - 2 year lease @ 1450 per month

I purchased the property for $75,000, and I thought the rehab would be about $20,000, so I borrowed $95,000 from a private money lender. On the day of closing, $75,000 was used for purchase. The remainder of the money was given to me after closing costs for the property's rehab. After paying closing costs, I received about $18,000 to use towards the rehab of the property. The closing of my first investment purchase was complete! I was on my way to the property, and I was so happy I had tears running down my face. When I got to the house, I sat there in silence, full of gratitude. I was so distracted that I didn't notice the musty smell in the house. I took out my phone and started to make some calls. It was time to start the rehab process!

The rehab process wasn't as bad as I thought. It was actually fun to learn, and I was able to complete the rehab on time and on budget. Once the rehab was complete, I reached out to a residential bank to refinance the property. These are longer-term loans by banks with competitive interest rates. The bank started the refinance process and eventually did an appraisal. I was nervous and was praying for a high appraisal. Two days later, I got a phone call that the appraisal was ready, and it was being sent to my email. I opened the email and was pleasantly surprised. The appraisal came in at $145,000! The bank offered me a loan amount of $108,000, and I owed my private money lender only $95,000. That meant I could actually pocket the remaining cash if I wanted!!! I chose only to borrow $100,000 because I would rather have a smaller monthly payment and more equity in the property. If I borrowed $108,000, my monthly payment would have been slightly higher, decreasing my net cash flow.

Let me explain this a little further.

If I borrow $100k, my loan payment, including taxes, principle, and interest, would be approximately $1,000 a month. If I borrow $108,000, it may come out to $1050 or $1100, depending on the loan terms. If I get $1450 in rent, my cash flow is $450 if I borrow $100,000. If I borrow $108,000, my cash flow may be around $400. Remember, the goal is to eventually pay down these properties, so the smaller the loan amount, the better. Once I closed on the refinance, the bank paid my lender off, and the refinance costs were covered with the loan amount. Pretty sweet deal, right?

Not only do I have $450 net cash flow coming in every month, but did you pay attention to the equity I have in the property? When I added up my costs, they totaled approximately $100,000, but my property appraised for $145,000!! That is $45,000 in equity. I could have sold the house and made a decent amount of cash, but my plan is to build long term wealth, so I kept the property and the equity and can collect the $450 cash flow every month for life (or as long as I hold onto the property). The best part is that there is ZERO money out of pocket!

It took me about four months to complete the entire transaction. Just to recap, these are the steps I took:

Step one - Got the property under contract and secured a lender.
Step two - Rehabbed the property once I closed on it.
Step three - Signed a lease and got a tenant in place.
Step four - Refinanced and paid off the lender.

Of course, there is a lot more that goes into it, but this process is repeatable!! And once you have a couple under your belt, you can do several deals at a time using the same or different private money lenders to scale up your portfolio!!

All the details that go into all of these processes were all taught in class, and if there was anything I was stuck on, my answer was just a phone call away. Best decision ever!

Real Estate Myth

4. I don't want to deal with tenants. I've heard they are always a problem.

Occasionally you may get a tenant that may be a problem. Still, quite honestly, most tenants I have experienced have been responsible and take pride in keeping up the house and making their payments on time. At times, a few may be a little late on rent, but they always make it a point to pay, and you can collect late fees on those based on your lease agreement. It's important to build a portfolio because if you have that one tenant that gives you a problem, it won't have a huge impact on your portfolio's performance.

Real Estate Investing Tip - When dealing with tenants, treat them how you would want to be treated. If an emergency repair arises, treat it as an emergency and get someone out there as soon as possible to handle it. Within non-emergency repairs, you have a little more time to work with as long as it's taken care of in a reasonable time period. Just like you want to get your rent paid on time, these tenants want their issues resolved in a timely manner.

CHAPTER FIVE

Feeling Frustrated
Why Can't I Get More Deals?

DO YOU EVER GET the feeling that people around you are doing so well and having success, and you're just lagging behind? Or maybe things work out for other people, but the same doesn't work out for you?

I am sure most people have felt this way at some point in their lives, and this is exactly how I felt, early on, in my journey of real estate investing. Although I got my first property fairly quickly, my next 2-3 properties took me a while to find. I walked through many properties and put in plenty of offers. They either didn't get accepted because someone else beat me to it, the property had some sort of issue that was too costly or risky to deal with, or it didn't meet my equity and cash flow standards once I spent more time calculating profits.

I started to feel like I wasn't good enough. I must have had beginner's luck with the first one. Investors around me were getting properties under contract left and right. A few of my friends who started investing with me already had 5-6 properties while I was still stuck at one. I started to get frustrated with myself and felt I was lagging behind. What was I doing wrong? Why couldn't I grow at a rate that others around me were? It was about a nine-month hiatus before I finally got my 2nd property.

Those nine months were mentally tough. I was trying and going to the meetings they had to stay connected with other investors but still no results until I realized about a year later what was actually happening during those nine months.

In hindsight, those nine months were a blessing in disguise!

"Life" was training me and getting me ready for what was to come. During those months, I physically looked at properties, calculated rehab amounts, did number analysis, put in offers, had to go through the feeling of getting a property under contract only to be strong enough emotionally to back away because the numbers weren't profitable. It was intense training that I didn't realize was happening. I used to be so intimidated just to put in an offer. There was something about putting in an offer that made me feel fearful.

After acquiring my second, third, and fourth properties, which happened to not be too far apart from each other, I realized that I got over my fear of putting in offers. I could walk a property within 15 minutes, estimate the rehab cost, do my cash flow analysis within five minutes and quickly get to my offer price. What took me a couple of hours to do before I could now do within 20 minutes. It felt amazing how much I learned and the progress I had made.

Let me give you an example of one of the properties I am proud of.

The property is in a town called Hanover Park. It's a three-bedroom, one-bathroom house with no basement and no garage. It has a driveway and a nice back yard, and it was presented to me by one of my business partners. We were planning to go 50/50.

As soon as I looked at the property online, I was able to assess what it was worth all fixed up. I used what I learned in class to calculate the After Repair Value (ARV), which was $150,000. I was able to calculate the ARV beforehand using tools online. It's always beneficial to have this number in mind before visiting the property.

I went to the property and calculated the rehab amount, which added up to $27,000. I had to replace the siding, the heating, and air conditioning, and everything else was cosmetic. The bathroom and the kitchen needed to be updated and the walls painted.

I like to have a minimum of 25% equity after the property is all fixed up, so if I take what the property is worth all fixed up ($160,000) and subtract that by $40.000 (the 25% equity of $160,000), It computes to $120,000. I know the rehab amount is $27,000, plus I allocate about $5,000 for closing costs, finance costs, and utilities. If I subtract $120,000 - $27,000 - $5,000, that comes out to $88,000. $88,000 should be my highest offer price. My business partner and I offered $75,000 to start with, and we were shocked when they accepted it! That's about $13,000 more in equity. I thought they would counter the offer, but they must have been in a rush to sell it.

This was definitely a home run deal because when I refinanced the property, I was able to pay the lender back completely and had some extra cash to pull out because the property appraised for $160,000. We decided to leave the extra equity in the property to have a lower loan balance.

Although I realized that life was training me to be a successful real estate investor, some of the other investors were still moving at a much faster rate. I was grateful for what I had been doing, but why couldn't I move as fast? Were they that much smarter than me? Was I not looking at properties fast enough? It was actually none of those. What I realized was that I had to move at my own pace based on my personal situation.

So what was the reason I wasn't doing ten deals a year?

I had no cash saved up; therefore, I had to be extremely picky with the properties. I had to make sure that rehab costs were as accurate as possible. I had to be conservative with the ARV that I calculated to make sure I could refinance enough money to pay back the private money lender with the refinance loan.

Other investors didn't have to be as conservative as I did because they had some capital or cash to work with. For example, if the rehab cost went over or if the property didn't appraise as expected, they were in a position to bring cash to closing. They didn't have to be as conservative with their numbers as I did, meaning they were able to get more deals because they had a safety net that I didn't have.

In the same example (Hanover Park property), if the property had appraised for $145,000, I would have had to bring about $5,000 to closing. At the time, I didn't have that luxury. Therefore I had to pass up many deals. Keep in mind, bringing $5,000 to the closing table is still a phenomenal investment. The net cash flow on this property is $700 per month. It is a no brainer to invest $5,000 of your own cash to make $700 per month. Today I would grab a deal like this in a heartbeat.

That was just one of the circumstances I had to work through. Working full-time had some limitations as well as being a single parent, but it's better to do a couple of deals a year than no deals at all! My time would come!

Real Estate Myth

5. Only buy when the market is hot.

Real estate can be purchased at any point in time regardless of if the market is hot or not, as long as the numbers are in line. There is a cycle to most things in life, including the market. If you're going to hold properties long term, your equity will fluctuate over time. Remember, you will still have the cash flow.

Real Estate Investing Tip- Pay attention to real estate cycles and price points on properties. For example, look at the property price in 2006 before the crash, when prices were highest, and compare them to 2009 to 2011. This was when they were at their low point. Compare the current price to where that falls on the scale. Pay attention to the real estate cycles during your era.

CHAPTER SIX

Life Happens- Overcoming the Hurdles

I WAS FINALLY STARTING to get the hang of things after completing my 4th property. I felt considerably more confident and eventually started seeing the momentum heading in the right direction. I received a 15% merit increase at work based on my performance, and it felt great. I could balance my full-time job, real estate investing, caring for the kids while increasingly getting better at juggling it all. The kids had adjusted to a routine, and it was nice that they were old enough to visit properties with me. We started to bond over real estate. They loved the before and after transformation of rehabs. My older son had also started working part-time at the company I was working for. Life was busy but good. I was consistently making progress, and the vision that once was a blur was coming into focus.

It was a nice summer day on June 14, 2016. I was still feeling elated from the news I received a few days prior that my offer got accepted. It was my fifth property under contract! This was a situation that I had not encountered before. A wholesaler actually reached out to me to see if I was interested after hearing from a friend that I had purchased a previous investment property. I guess word can get around, and I did not mind because it worked out in my favor. That is when I first realized that you don't necessarily have to go chasing properties all the time. They can also come to you.

I was sitting in my office, reviewing some updates to a business requirement for a project I was heading, when I received a call at my extension from the HR manager. She asked me if I could come down to her office. I quickly hung up and wondered if something happened to one of my employees. At the time, I had more than 80 people under my watch, and from time to time, there would be some employee issue that needed attention.

I grabbed my notebook, walked down the hall, down the stairs, and took a seat in the chair. The HR manager shut the door behind me—it was just her and I in the room. I sat there for a few moments waiting for her to speak. She finally started to talk, and my brain froze. I could not process anything beyond what she just told me. I sat there for about 5 seconds staring at her because I wasn't sure if what she said was real.

I asked her to repeat herself, and she started to speak and present me with some paperwork. I stopped her and told her there must be some misunderstanding.

I had just received one of the biggest shocks of my life. They were letting me go from the company! A company that I was at for 15 years!

A company that I received five promotions at in a span of 10 years! A company that recently gave me a 15% pay increase for outstanding performance!

With a look of confusion, I asked her why she was letting me go. She gave me some response about me not following up with a vendor who had a deadline to send us a file at 9 am that day. I told her I didn't send an email because at 8:50 am when I still had not received the file, I picked up the phone and called the vendor instead. That was a more viable option because I could get someone live on the phone to handle it immediately rather than waiting on a response via email. I also told her she could check my phone records as proof. She sat there looking at me dumbfounded and did not know how to respond. I asked her where my manager was and why she wasn't in this room. Shouldn't she be here in the room with me if I was being let go? The HR manager did not know what to say, so she called my manager and asked her if she could come down to her office.

After waiting in the room for a few minutes, I heard the door creak open, and there she was with a confused and worried look. When I confronted her about why I was being let go and told her about the phone call, she had that similar dumbfounded expression. I guess she didn't think about the phone call option. She was too focused on email. Suddenly I became aware of what was happening. It started to click. Her changed behavior over the past few months now made sense. I felt it, and now I knew. She no longer wanted me there.

I think what hurt me most about this whole situation was her insensitivity to my situation and our relationship. I worked under her for more than 15 years. She gave me promotion after promotion because of my hard work and dedication over the years. She told people I was her right hand. I outworked others to get a management position so that I had enough to provide for my kids. She and I had been to each other's houses for social gatherings. We would go exercise together and share our personal stories. She knew I was a single mother who had to support the kids on my own.

What did I do to deserve this? If I did something, why didn't she give me any warnings, either written or verbal? Why was I made to seem that I was doing a great job? Why did I receive a huge pay increase a few months prior? Why were other department heads praising my work? None of this made any sense to me.

When I realized she no longer wanted me, I took it personally and stopped asking questions. I went back to my office, grabbed my purse and keys, and left. I asked if I could come and take my belongings the following day, which they agreed to. I sat in my car for about an hour in the parking lot with tears rolling down my eyes non-stop. I drove home wondering what I was going to tell my kids, especially the older one who worked at the same company. It was an extremely emotional moment for me. I felt weak telling my kids I didn't have a job. I didn't want them to worry, and I didn't want them to feel insecure.

I finally conjured up the strength to tell the kids. I told my older son first because he worked there. I was mature about it and explained to him that what happened to me and his role at the company were unrelated and that he would not be affected. He still had a choice to work there if he wanted.

That evening I did receive a six-month severance letter from the HR department to keep the peace with the company. It was a bit of relief. However, I knew my job was specialized and that it would take me some time to find work in the same field.

It took me a few months to get over the pain and hurt I felt. I would wake up around 3 am every night and sit on my deck, and cry. It was dark outside, and no one could see nor hear me cry. I took it really personally because my boss was like a second mother to me in the workplace. Don't get me wrong, she was only a few years older than I was, but she taught me so much over the past decade and a half. I really admired the way she kept everyone on their toes and her dedication to the company. I felt rejected, confused, worried, disappointed, sad, embarrassed, and the list goes on. Even though I had not done anything to be embarrassed about, it was difficult to tell my friends and some of my co-workers that I got let go. I am sure people assumed something major must have happened, even though that wasn't the case. I did decide not to tell my parents. My dad had some health issues, and my mom and older sister were taking care of him, and I didn't want to burden them with the news. I did not want them to worry. I was going to figure this out on my own.

With all these drastic, sudden changes, I now had another issue to worry about. How was I going to refinance my properties with no income? I felt my real estate career was over. I had just acquired my 5th property, and now, I didn't know what to do,

Despite all the feelings I was going through, I had to be strong for myself and my children, so after some time, in misery, I got up and started revamping my resume and put myself out in the market to seek new employment.

So what was I going to do with that 5th property? Based on the situation, I decided to flip it, and I partnered with another student who could help me with the rehab portion. I wasn't sure how long I would be out of work, and I may need to use the profit from the flip to live off of.

For those of you who are new to real estate, the definition of a flip is: Purchasing a property and improving it so that it is in livable condition and simultaneously increasing the property's value and selling it for a profit.

The numbers of this property are as follows:

Purchase price was $46,000.
The rehab amount was $45,000.
The amount it sold for was $133,000.

The rehab work was my partner's responsibility. I was able to get a private money lender because I was still considered a student of the mastery education course, and they were happy to arrange a lender because it met the lending standards.

That year, I did my very first flip. It took a total of about five months to do the rehab and sell it. I was still out of a job, and just as I predicted, my severance was close to running out. I was down to my last couple thousand dollars. I was so relieved when we found a buyer and the property was under contract. For the very first time, I was the seller instead of the buyer. The property officially sold in December 2016, and we finally got our proceeds at the closing table. It wasn't as much as I originally imagined because the rehab went over budget and we held it a couple months longer than anticipated. However, I was extremely grateful because the profit I made after I split it with my partner would keep me afloat for a few more months.

The profit gave me a safety net and made me feel a sense of financial security for the time being. It also gave me my first experience with a flip. The next time I did a flip, I was sure I would do better. I was in the mode of rehabbing rentals, and it slipped my mind that flip rehabs were done differently, and I didn't keep an eye on my partner the way I should have. I didn't beat myself up for it because it's part of the learning process—I had learned from my mistakes.

A strategy I could have used to make a little more profit was to wait a few months and sell it in February instead of December. The project was completed in November, but because of my desperate situation, I decided to put it on the market right away and accept the offer so that I had some funds. If I'd had a job, I would have waited a few months when there were more buyers in the early spring market.

I realized that real estate can work in any situation. I started investing in rentals, but I had no income, so I changed my strategy for property #5 to a flip based on my personal circumstances. If I had not needed the cash, I could have kept it as a rental even with no employment. When my mentor advised me that I could still keep it as a rental and refinance using the commercial route, it was an eye-opening conversation. Of course, I was too embarrassed to tell my mentor I would be down to my last couple thousand dollars soon, so I nodded my head and changed the subject. I realized at that moment what that meant. It meant that I could continue doing rentals without a job using a commercial loan if I wanted. Maybe my real estate career wasn't over after all. Worst case scenario, I could find freelance projects and make some money to survive but continue to build my portfolio. There was hope again! It's comforting to know that there are options in any situation. It doesn't matter how many wrenches life throws at you, real estate will always welcome you.

I felt extremely grateful and blessed that I was investing in real estate. Can you imagine if I had not had real estate to rely on as a backup? I am not the type of person that likes to borrow money from family or friends. I would have been completely devastated if it ever came to that point.

Some people have asked me why I decided to partner on the deal instead of keeping it all to myself. Now that I think about it, I probably could have pulled it off on my own, but at the time, I chose to give up 40% of the profit so that I didn't have to manage the rehab. This allowed me to have some time open to continue looking for jobs and go on interviews and have someone who was more experienced than I was at rehabs to learn from.

Some of you may be curious about how I structured this partnership so let's go through this.

In a flip partnership, the key pieces are the following:

- Finding the deal and getting the deal under contract
- Funding
- Rehabbing

In this example, I got the property under contract, and I arranged the funding. My partner was responsible for the rehab. This included pulling permits and dealing with the village for inspections.

I got a private money lender to fund the purchase and rehab.

In this partnership, I negotiated 60% of the net profit, and my partner took 40%. This was a good deal for him because he knew I could have hired a contractor to do the job. 40% was a good chunk of change for my partner, so it was a win-win.

Real Estate Myth

6. Partnerships have to be 50/50.

Partnerships can be formed in any way but just keep in mind to be fair. At times, some people may be willing to take less profit on a deal when working with an experienced investor because the novice investor gains experience, which is priceless. Always consider what expertise and key pieces each of you is bringing to the table. The goal is always to keep good relationships. You never know when the other person may present you with a great deal.

Consider some of these partnership scenarios:

Investor and Contractor
Investor and Lender
Investor who works full time vs. Investor who has time
Investor with experience vs. novice investor
Why might these be good partnerships?

An investor partnering with a contractor can mean less labor costs. The contractor can do the rehab at his cost with no profit and share the profit after the property sells or share the cash flow if they decide to keep it as a rental.

An investor and lender can be a great partnership because the lender may bring all or some of the money to the deal, saving on points and interest fees, resulting in more net profit.

An investor who works full-time will probably lack time as a resource, so it may be wise to invest with a partner who can manage the day to day items on the property, such as checking on the rehab, working with the villages, arranging insurance, utilities, etc.

An investor with experience may partner with a novice investor as long as that investor brings value to the deal. It could be either bringing funds or having the deal under contract. The novice investor gets to work with an experienced investor, which equates to less risk and the opportunity to gain experience.

Real Estate Investing Tip - When partnering, make sure you have a joint venture agreement in place. This explains who is responsible for what and how the deal will be conducted and the exit strategy. This should be done regardless of the relationship. Business is business.

CHAPTER SEVEN

On Fire

AFTER ABOUT NINE MONTHS of being unemployed, I finally found a position to my liking, which complimented my experience. I was extremely grateful the day I got offered the job. It was in downtown Chicago, which meant I had to take the train and then walk 25 minutes each way, which made my total commute to 3 hours daily. I didn't mind because I had peace of mind knowing I had stable income.

The nice part about the job was that it wasn't as stressful as my previous job, and I wasn't in meetings 80% of my day, which gave me time to think.

Something happened that year. It was like everything I had been learning came together at once, and I was on fire! That year, I did nine rentals! I was in the zone and kept going. I would get properties under contract to the point that I would actually stop looking for new deals because I had properties in abundance.

The saying, "If you keep at it long enough, it will all come to fruition," holds a lot of truth. All the stress and sadness I endured after

I lost my job was worth it because there was no way I would have been able to acquire nine rentals with my previous job. Everything happens for a reason, and I truly believe in that.

In this chapter, I want to get more into how the properties were acquired, what steps were used, and an analysis of each deal. We will go through five examples of properties I have purchased during this year. I will list the town and the average household income to give you an idea of the area. In the example, if I use the term "other costs," this refers to financing, utilities, and taxes until the refinance is complete. In these examples, the equity is calculated by subtracting the After Repair Value (ARV) from the purchase price, rehab, and holding costs.

Example 1

Property Location - Bridgeview, IL
Average Household Income = $51,270
Bed/Bath = 3 bedroom/1.5 bath
Square feet - 1330
Purchase price = $90,000
Rehab = $24,450
Other costs = $3,500
After repair value = $160,000
Loan amount = $117,000
Equity - $42,050
Monthly mortgage, including taxes and insurance = $1200
Monthly rent = $1750
Monthly Net Cash flow = $550

This property was listed as a short-sale on the MLS. The rehab was fairly easy—no unexpected surprises during the rehab. The property appraised close to the projected value, so I only had to use about $3,000 of my own cash to cover refinancing, costs, and interest to the private money lender (PVM). The bank paid the PVM loan in full. I originally borrowed $115,000, and $90,000 was used to purchase the property, and the rest was used for rehab.

Pros - Solid brick house with a great layout. Very easy to rent due to demand for rentals in this area.

Cons - There were some electrical lines close to the backyard, so the property appraised for $5,000 less than I initially projected.

Example 2

Property Location - Hillside, IL

Average household income = $52,175

Bed/bath = 2 bedroom/1.5 bath

Square feet - 833 (has a basement)

Purchase price = $76,000

Rehab = $36,000

Other costs = $4,000

After repair value = $145,000

Loan amount = $108,000

Equity - $29,,000

Monthly mortgage, including taxes and insurance = $1050Monthly rent = $1485

Monthly Net Cash flow = $435

This property was listed on the market. I was lucky enough to be one of the first to look at the property and get my offer in. I borrowed $105,000 from the private money lender. I originally thought the rehab would be $30,000, but I ended up having to spend about $5,000 more. The rehab on this was extensive, but it didn't scare me away.

There was something interesting that happened on this property. I originally had the contract for $80,000, but while the property was under contract, there was a rainstorm, and there was about two feet of water in the basement. We found out that the electricity was cut for some reason, which stopped the sump pump from working. The water must have been sitting there for a few weeks because when we went into the property to do a walk-thru, there was an extensive amount of mold in the basement.

We negotiated with the seller, and they agreed to lower it by $3,000 due to unforeseen circumstances. Although I got the price reduced, I ended up getting rid of all the drywall and turned it into an unfinished basement rather than finished, which would have added more costs. In that area, an unfinished basement is common and used mainly for storage purposes, so the decision made sense. Not to mention that it's viable from a rental perspective because sometimes basements can get a little bit of water, and if it's unfinished, there is less exposure to damage, which means decreased costs.

Pros - Great, stable area, with demand for rentals due to it being near the highway on the way to downtown Chicago

Cons- Square footage is rather small. Ideal for 1-3 people

Example 3

Property Location - Justice, IL

Average household income = $52,203

Bed/bath = 2 bedroom/1 bath per unit. This is a multi-unit, two-unit home.

Square feet = 1848 total. Each unit is 924 square feet, Full unfinished basement.

Purchase price = $148,000

Rehab = $45,000

Other costs = $6,000

After repair value = $256,000

Loan amount = $190,000

Equity - $57,000

Monthly mortgage, including taxes and insurance = $1757

Monthly rent = $1300 per unit = $2600 total

Monthly Net Cash flow = $843

This property was my first multi-unit. I thought a multi-unit would be a vastly different experience, but that was not the case. This was also listed on the MLS and a friend, who owed me a huge favor, pointed this property out to me. This two-unit property had identical layouts in each unit. I had estimated the rehab cost to be lower. I hired a new contractor because my original contractor was already working on a few of my other properties, and I didn't want to slow him down. The issue I ran into was that he wasn't as experienced as I thought.

After a few weeks, my friend that was with me noticed that something was off. The work started wasn't done properly, and clearly, this contractor did not know what he was doing. For example, he was supposed to install a cement board in the shower area but failed to do so. I had to fire the contractor and start all over again. I lost about

$6,000. That loss in the bigger scheme of things was minimal because had the issue not been identified, it would have resulted in costly issues down the road. It's better to cut your losses early to avoid major problems in the future.

I ended up putting my original contractor back on it. It took a bit longer, but I didn't have to worry about poor craftsmanship.

Pros: Two units in one location reduces costs.

Cons - The village requires an annual pest inspection report. This is an added cost that is unnecessary for the landlord, especially if there haven't been any issues.

Example 4

Property Location - Streamwood, IL
Average household income = $72,720
Bed/bath = 3 bedroom/1 bath per unit
Square feet = 1132 total - no basement and attached garage
Purchase price = $78,000
Rehab = $40,000
Other costs = $5,500
After repair value = $180,000
Loan amount = $111,000
Equity - $56,500
Monthly mortgage, including taxes and insurance = $1100
Monthly rent = $1700
Monthly Net Cash flow = $600

When I first walked into this property, it reeked like pet urine everywhere. I had to hold my breath while I was viewing the property. The house was not in good shape, but it was a simple enough house to estimate the rehab costs. We had to be really careful because the garage you see attached was made into a 4th bedroom illegally. This was an off-market deal. A friend of mine found the property and asked me if I wanted to partner with him. He was unemployed at the time, and I had W-2 income, which would make it easy to refinance with a residential loan.

The sellers were trying to sell this property to us as a four-bedroom dwelling, but I learned in mastery class that this particular village was very strict. It was possible that they may require us to convert that 4th bedroom back to a garage during inspection.

After we got the property under contract, we decided to get village officials out there to do a pre-inspection because we wanted to do our complete due diligence. Sure enough, the inspector came out and said it was an illegal 4th bedroom and that we either had to make it a legal bedroom and add a garage on the other side of the house or convert it back to a garage and keep it as a three-bedroom.

Once we got this report, we took it to the sellers and negotiated the price down since it was no longer four legal bedrooms. We were able to negotiate the price in our favor, which made it a much better deal than what we anticipated. Overall, the property went reasonably well, and we were able to rent it out fairly quickly. Sometimes what we perceive as hurdles can be blessings in disguise.

Pros - Hot rental area and likelihood of long term tenants.

Cons - No cons with the property.

Example 5

Property Location - Evergreen Park, IL
Average household income = $65,744
Bed/bath = 3 bedroom/1 bath per unit
Square feet =1250
Purchase price = $105,000
Rehab = $15,000
Other costs = $2,000
After repair value = $150,000
Loan amount = $120,000

Equity - $28,000

Monthly mortgage, including taxes and insurance = $1100

Monthly rent = $1600

Monthly Net Cash flow = $500

The property was listed on the MLS, and as soon as I noticed it, I jumped on it. Based on the pictures, the property looked in great condition. I rushed to the property and had it under contract within a couple of hours after listing it. It was the quickest property I got under contract. This was also one of my quickest rehabs. The property was in great shape when I purchased it. I decided to change it from boiler heating to central air; otherwise, the rehab amount would have been significantly lower. I did have a few hiccups on this property after I rented it. Somehow there was a leak that caused a high amount of water to go underneath the house. The tenants said they didn't hear or see anything.

All of a sudden, the village came in and turned off the water. When the tenants notified me that there was no water, I called the village, and they said there is some massive water leak, and their meter showed $3,000 worth of water used. I was so confused, and it took a while to figure out what was happening. I got a plumber in there, and he said I should just remove the boiler unit altogether because that was what caused it. It had not been used since I got a new furnace and air conditioner. I had to pay the $3,000 because the village would not budge. The issue never occurred again, and the property has been doing well since.

Lessons learned - Sometimes properties look great on the surface but may have issues that we cannot see. It is a good idea to get an inspection report so that you can minimize your risk.

Pros - Great, solid investment area

Cons - The property appraised about $10k lower than expected because it was very close to a railroad track. In my excitement over how great the property looked, I failed to notice the railroad tracks right next to it. Still, it was a great investment property.

You should notice a trend in the type of properties I personally invest in. Those are the money makers and are some of the safest risks. Properties in those markets tend to rent fairly quickly because they cater to the renting population. For example, if you rent out in an affluent area, you may find that it may take a little more time to rent because the renters' pool is less. Affluent neighborhoods tend to have more homeowner populations.

Real Estate Myth

7. Real estate is easy passive income.

Investing in real estate works, but you MUST do it the correct way, and you MUST put work into it. There are definitely ways to make it easier on you by having property managers, contractors managing the rehab, and people to run errands, but that will have a slight impact on your expenses.

Real Estate Investing Tip - Pay attention to where you are spending time during the real estate investing process. During the initial learning process, you may have to invest time in all areas to learn it, but once you get the hang of it, the best use of your time will be on property acquisition. If you're spending too much time managing your rehab and not enough time acquiring properties, you might want to consider hiring a good contractor.

CHAPTER EIGHT

Reached Huge Milestone - 25 Properties

THE NEXT COUPLE OF YEARS flew by. *Purchase - rehab - rent - refinance. Purchase - rehab - rent - refinance*—repeating the process until I reached my goal. Once you get a few properties under your belt, you feel a high each time you hear the words "your offer has been accepted" or "clear to close." If a month went by, and I didn't hear those words, I would start feeling like I was getting left behind, so I would work a bit harder till I heard those words again. Finally, I did it! I got my 25th property under contract in a small suburb of Chicago - Alsip, IL. It was a three-bedroom, two-bath home with a full basement.

I felt like I could finally take a break from this marathon I was running and felt extremely grateful that I had achieved my goal. I am not sure where the number 25 actually came from. My original goal when I first joined the mastery class was to have five properties. Once I got that five, it turned into ten and then full-time to 15 and so on. When I realized I could retire off of real estate, I kept going until I felt I had a comfortable amount of monthly cash flow.

After hitting 25 rentals, I decided that I would focus more on flips so that I could take those profits and start paying off the loans. Although I can continue to build my rental portfolio, I've decided that having some free and clear properties would give me some peace of mind.

I was at dinner having a conversation with one of my friends, and in conversation, it came up that I had a multi-million dollar portfolio. Although I knew that was what I was building, it truly didn't hit me till that evening. I was so busy building the portfolio that I didn't realize what each property I was acquiring was doing for me. I didn't put it into perspective till that evening. Let me share with you exactly what that means.

We will start with the numbers first. On average, each property has a $500 monthly net cash flow. This is after all expenses such as mortgage, interest, taxes, and insurance.

Cash flow

$500 * 25 properties = $12,500 net monthly cash flow
12,500 * 12 = $150,000 annual net cash flow

Equity

Let's say that each property, on average, is worth $160,000.
Let's say that I have an average of 30% equity for each property.
$160,000 x .30 = 48,000
$48,000 x 25 = $1.2M

The equity in the portfolio is $1.2 Million. When the properties are all paid off, it will be approximately $4 million. Keep in mind that the value of the properties fluctuates based on the market. This scenario is being used as an example to help put the numbers into perspective.

Now let's take a look at how these numbers impact our lives:

- The net cash flow replaces a decent household income, which means you can quit your job and live off your passive income.
- In difficult times, you can sell a property for cash if you need to.

Payoff all those loans, and now you only have to worry about taxes and insurance. In this example, you would be netting about $25,000 per month. I can think of many ways to spend that money. Basically, you have the resources to do what you please.

Welcome to the path of freedom!

Aside from the 25 rentals, I have partnered in over 20 real estate transactions in years 3 and 4 of my investing career. I was getting properties under contract, and I shared them with other investors I was friends with. It helped to pay off my school debt and helped them accumulate rentals in their portfolio. It was a win-win

Real Estate Myth

8. I can't do residential refinancing on investment properties.

You can refinance your investment properties with residential loans. There is a limit to how many you can do, and this number is approximately 8-10.

Real Estate Investing Tip - Take advantage of the residential loans on your investment properties. Rates are much lower, which increases your cash flow, and terms are generally longer. You should check with your bank as terms and loan types are changing.

CHAPTER NINE

The Magic of Building a Team

IF SOMEONE WERE TO ask me what attributed to my success with investing, I would have to say one of the biggest factors to my success is the team I built. Being able to do ten properties a year as a working full time mother would not be possible without assembling the right team. Real estate investing is not something you will succeed at by doing it alone.

Assembling the right team comes with time and experience. I was fortunate enough to have a built-in support team when I joined the real estate mastery classes. They had experienced attorneys, accountants, lenders, tradespeople, and so much more. They knew exactly what we did and knew how to handle complex files or situations. During my journey, I formed a real estate team of my own that became like a 2nd family after working together on numerous transactions. My main team consisted of:

My mentors and supporting friends who invest
Contractor and other Tradesman
Attorney

Leasing agent and misc errands
Lenders

Once you work with your team on a few transactions, the process becomes much smoother, and you continue to build trust. For example, at one point, I would have to put together a full lending proposal to my lenders when I needed money for a project. Upon building a rapport and repeated successful transactions, they no longer required a proposal. Similarly, my contractor knows exactly what needs to be done when it comes to rehabs. The paint colors, type of flooring, the quality level of rehabs. Because of the level of trust over time, there is no need for me to check on my properties every week. He tells me when he needs a payment, and I trust that the work is done. In no way do I recommend working this way until a level of trust is developed, and trust can take a few years to build. When I first started investing, I would check on my properties on average once per week.

Once the property is complete, I have another team member who does showings on the property to potential tenants. I have no problem giving up the commission because my time is better spent on acquiring more properties. In addition, he takes care of tasks such as registering rentals with the village and other miscellaneous tasks associated with the properties.

Having your own team is crucial to the success of real estate investing. What is important is that you respect each person for what they do and pay them what was agreed upon. There will be instances where you may have to extend your loan, or perhaps something in the scope of work was missed, but at the end of the day, you need to realize that this is part of real estate and can be worked through in a fair manner.

Having a great support team and mentor is crucial to your success. You should learn from someone who has done what you want to achieve. They can pave the way for you through their own experiences, and doing it this way will minimize risks and provide a greater opportunity to succeed.

My mentor and supporting friends are always there to run deals past when I need a second pair of eyes, or perhaps someone knows an area much better than I do, so I reach out to them for advice.

My attorney keeps an eye out to ensure my earnest money is protected and is looking out for any red flags. Everyone is working in my best interest. It feels like there's a safety net waiting to catch me if I fall. I never feel alone.

When you have a great team, you can invest from anywhere. Take my younger sister, for example, the one that lives out in California. Talk about how lucky she is! She recently purchased an investment property near the Chicago area based on my recommendation. She was able to take advantage of the team I built over time to purchase, rehab and is now in the process of having my leasing agent find her a tenant. She will have over $40,000 equity and more than $600 monthly cash flow in this property, all while sitting in the comfort of her home in California. How is this possible? By having the right resources and building a team. The perks of having a family member in real estate willing to help is definitely an added plus. We joke about how she owes me big time. All jokes aside, it feels good when the people closest to you benefit.

I am planning on diversifying and purchasing investment properties in a couple of other states. I am doing my area analysis and looking for people to connect with to start building my team. It's definitely something I am excited about and looking forward to.

Real Estate Myth

9. Having too many home loans is bad for my credit and taxes.

Owning real estate does not hurt your credit, nor does it impact your taxes negatively. Remember, there are tax breaks for investors. Having positive cash flow on a rental property even with a loan is looked at positively because it is an income-producing asset.

Real Estate Investing Tip - Get to know your accountant and attorney and build a good relationship with them. Remember to choose an attorney and accountant who are experienced working with real estate investors. They are a part of your real estate investing team and can give you sound advice throughout the process to maximize your profits without compromising integrity.

CHAPTER TEN

Next Steps and What's Stopping You

BUILDING WEALTH THROUGH real estate has been a life-changing process for me. I have been able to do things I hadn't dreamt of. I realized that many people live their entire lives trying to acquire one resource–Money. You need money to live, and unfortunately, most of us spend the bulk of our lives trying to acquire it for ourselves and our loved ones.

Imagine if you no longer have to spend a significant portion of your life chasing money. What would you do with the rest of your time? There is so much out there to experience and enjoy. Most people never get to experience what is out there because they are living a routine lifestyle, which limits time for other experiences. People don't remember the monotony in their lives. They remember the ability to experience life in all that it has to offer, and that is what I define as rich!

It took me many years to realize what being rich was. It's not necessarily having a certain amount of money in your bank account, although that is something that you need to work on as quickly as possible so you can focus on the bigger picture of living life. If you haven't already done so, you need to start now to create a nest egg that will take care of you for life.

As I explained earlier, it doesn't matter what situation you are in. There is hope for every single one of you. The only difference is that some may achieve their goals sooner than others, depending on your personal situation. Do not let limiting beliefs impede your growth.

If you feel or believe you can't do it or that it works for everyone else but not for you, then you must work on your limiting mindset.

If you have little money, it can still work for you. Remember, as long as the deal makes sense, there are lenders out there willing to fund all or most of the transaction. You will need to invest in the right education and mentors.

If you have no time, you will have to change things up a little to prioritize to make time, but you don't need to spend all day on it to be successful. In the beginning stages, you may need to put aside about 10 hours per week to learn and practice. As you become more experienced and skilled, you can choose to spend less time.

If you don't have knowledge or experience, no need to worry. I had absolutely no knowledge or experience with investing when I started. There is plenty of information out there that is helpful and will help you get started. You can also join groups that will be a support system throughout your investing career. There are courses that cost money, and there are meetings that are absolutely free. Real estate does not discriminate.

If you have bad credit, debt, or are in any adverse situations, you can always work towards starting to make those situations better. There is help out there. It may take you a little bit longer to dig yourself out of a hole. Intention and action are key.

I can now say with conviction that there is something for everyone. I have experienced this in my personal life and had a variety of setbacks and challenging situations that I had to overcome, and I realized that you need to do the best you can do and leave it at that. Opportunities start to chase you. Some you can't see immediately, but over time, your focus begins to become clearer, and you will be able to start seeing and feeling them when they appear.

When I said I am now living experiences I have never dreamt of, I am not talking about purchasing a luxury car or buying expensive purses, clothing, and shoes (which is also nice!).

I am talking about those experiences that are etched in my memories so that at any point, I can go back and access these memories, allowing me to stay in the feeling of gratitude and love.

I have been able to visit different countries and learn and experience other cultures and try a variety of other foods. Traveling to different places does add to the experiences of life. We also travel quite a bit domestically, exploring the United States.

Freeing up my time has allowed me to be more physically active. A group of real estate investors who have become dear friends all go hiking together in different parts of the U.S. My most memorable experience is hiking down and back up the Grand Canyon, which was about a 17-mile hike. It was definitely challenging but one of the most picturesque views I have seen.

In early 2019, I helped co-found WE WIN, LLC (Women Entrepreneurs Women Investment Network) with a couple of my friends who also invest in real estate. We saw the success that many women were achieving in real estate, and we decided to hold a platform where we could provide some guidance and education to inspire and motivate other women. We have inspired so many women and sometimes even men who have started building their real estate portfolios.

In August 2019, I went on a pilgrimage to Saudi Arabia as part of my Spiritual obligation called Hajj. I thought it was something that I would probably do later on in life, but I was able to go earlier than expected because of my financial situation. My sisters were also with me, but what I was so grateful for was that I was able to take my two teenage boys, something not many get to experience at that age.

Despite the amount of wealth, there will inevitably be times we feel down or low at some points in our lives. On March 7th, 2020, while I was at one of the mastery classes showing my property that I was flipping in Joliet, IL, I got that dreadful phone call that no one wants to hear.

My younger sister called me and told me our Dad was being rushed to the emergency room. He hadn't been feeling well the past couple of days to the point that he didn't have much energy to lift his hand to eat anything. My sister and I both took turns feeding him. My Dad had just come from Florida to visit while my mom was on her way to California to help my sister with the birth of her baby girl.

I notified my friend that I needed to leave class. I ran to the car and rushed to the hospital. When I got there, they were trying to revive him after multiple cardiac arrests. I remember hoping and praying in the hospital waiting room that he would make it. I thought to myself, *why wouldn't he?* He made it the last time, four years prior, when he had a fall that injured his brain. Back then, I got the call from my older sister in Florida saying that the doctors were already preparing us for a funeral. Well, he pulled through, and the doctors were shocked. They said it was a miracle that he was alive. I remember us praying persistently in that hospital room. So why wouldn't the prayers work this time?

Well, this time was different. He passed the same day. It was his time, but I was so grateful that he was able to live those extra four years the way he did. He was extremely happy and did not have a complaint about anything. Because of the fall, he struggled a bit with comprehension and mobility, and that is why I never mentioned the real estate investments to him. I don't know if he would have understood. I wish I had written this book earlier. I know he would have visually seen and held the book and would have been really proud of my accomplishments. I still yearn to see what his reaction would have been.

In early 2020, as soon as the COVID-19 virus started affecting lives, a few of my friends and I started the WE WIN FOUNDATION, a non-profit that helps local communities. Throughout 2020, we fed thousands of families in the local communities by setting up food distribution events and providing some rental assistance to those in need. It was our way of giving back to our communities, and it felt wonderful to be able to help in any way that we could. To this day, we continue to plan events to help in any way that we can.

In late 2020, I started doing something that I have always wanted to do–write a book. I didn't know how or what topic I would write on, but the idea came to me while we were all quarantined during Covid-19. I thought it would be helpful to share my story and the process I went through to achieve what I have today so that I may be able to inspire others.

I haven't stopped investing. Real estate is now in my blood and DNA. On occasion, I keep a property as a rental while working on flips. I currently have three flips going at once and one rental as I am completing this book. I enjoy watching other people grow their real estate portfolios. We all cheer each other on. We have each other's back and continue to move forward. I really wish more people could see what I see.

Real Estate Myth

10. I can learn real estate on my own. There is so much information out there. I can put the pieces together.

Although there is a significant amount of information out there, it is difficult to discern what works for you. It can take a significant amount of time, and your ability to scale up will be limited. You may be at a high risk of making mistakes that will eat away your profits. Getting the right education and support can make a vast difference in the quality of your real estate experience. Having lenders around you, real estate experts in all fields and someone you can ask questions is priceless. Education courses can be a bit pricey, but you can make that money back by doing just one deal.

Real Estate Tip - Make the decision and get started. Even if it's something like taking a free webinar, you won't know what you're missing until you start. Do it for your family, but most importantly for you!

Conclusion

THANK YOU TO ALL THE READERS who purchased the book and took the time to read it. I hope you enjoyed it and that it was able to help in some way. If you would like to get more information on the next steps, please email rei@farrahali.org Please share this with family or friends or encourage them to get a copy. A percentage of all proceeds will be going to the non-profit, We Win Foundation. Let's all win together!

Glossary of Frequently Used Real Estate Terms

Wholesale - contracting a home with a seller and finding a buyer at a higher price to keep the difference as a profit

Flip - Purchasing an asset and reselling it quickly for a profit. The property may need to be repaired or updated to sell for a profit.

Rental - Property from which the owner receives a monthly payment from a tenant to occupy the property.

Equity - The difference between the present market value of the property compared to what is owed to a lender or mortgage.

As-is - Listed for sale in its current state. The property will be sold without addressing any repairs or issues.

Refinance - Obtaining a new loan to pay off an existing mortgage or loan. This is usually done to get better terms and/or obtain a longer-term loan.

Hard money loan - Asset-based loans are usually used to fund a purchase, rehab, or both. Interest rates are typically higher than conventional loans.

Private money lender - Asset-based loan issued by an individual to finance a purchase, rehab, or a combination of both. The loan is usually secured by the property.

Appraisal - A professional opinion of the value of a home conducted by an appraiser. An appraiser uses comparables of homes sold and listed of similar type homes in close proximity to obtain the value.

Net cash flow - The amount of money an investor can pocket at the end of each month after payment of all expenses, including any mortgage or loan payments. Cash flow can be positive or negative.

Appreciation - Increase in the value of real estate property over time. An increase in value can be due to inflation, increased demand, or low supply.

Debt-to-income ratio - A personal finance measure used to compare monthly debt payment to the monthly gross income. Lenders use this metric to measure the ability to manage debt payments.

Cash on Cash return - Ratio of annual cash flow before tax to the total cash invested. This metric allows investors to assess the cash flows from their income-generating assets.

Off-Market property - A property that is being offered or purchased without public knowledge. These are not listed on public sites or the MLS for sale.

Real estate agent - A licensed professional that represents sellers or buyers in a real estate transaction. A real estate agent usually works under a licensed broker.

Real estate broker - A licensed professional who represents buyers and sellers of real estate and can work independently.

Real estate investor - Ownership of real estate for profit. This can be flipped for a quick profit or held over a period of time to produce income from tenants to build long term wealth.

THANK YOU FOR READING MY BOOK!

DOWNLOAD YOUR FREE GIFTS

Read This First

Just to say thanks for buying and reading my book, I would like to give you a 100% bonus gift for FREE, no strings attached!

To Download Now, Visit:
www.FarrahAli.org/freegift

I appreciate your interest in my book, and I value your feedback as it helps me improve future versions of this book. I would appreciate it if you could leave your invaluable review on Amazon.com with your feedback. Thank you!

Made in the USA
Middletown, DE
16 March 2021